little dark

Also by Karen Brennan

Poems:

Here on Earth (1989)
The Real Enough World (2005)

Fiction:

Wild Desire (1990)
The Garden in Which I Walk (2004)

Memoir:

Being with Rachel (2002)

little dark

Karen Brennan

Four Way Books
Tribeca

Please direct all inquiries to:
Editorial Office
Four Way Books
POB 535, Village Station
New York, NY 10014
www.fourwaybooks.com

Library of Congress Cataloging-in-Publication Data

Brennan, Karen, date
[Poems. Selections]
little dark / Karen Brennan.
pages cm
ISBN 978-1-935536-42-0 (alk. paper)
I. Title.
PS3552.R378L58 2014
811'.54--dc23
2013036109

This book is manufactured in the United States of America and printed on acid-free paper.

Four Way Books is a not-for-profit literary press. We are grateful for the assistance
we receive from individual donors, public arts agencies, and private foundations.

This publication is made possible with public funds from the National Endowment for the Arts.

and from the New York State Council on the Arts, a state agency.

We are a proud member
of the Council of Literary Magazines and Presses.

Distributed by University Press of New England
One Court Street, Lebanon, NH 03766

CONTENTS

For Stephen

with love

My hand astonishes me being full of spaces // the world framed within

Nature

Turn on the lights
Now that you are so far
Freeway miles towers rising from dispirited hills
Is this the nature of terror

Ballares

My room beaming in the dark I began my journey as if
Trees were furniture

I never believed in anything I walked through walls
Like Jesus

The children believed in me which still causes heartache

I made my way in my various names I skipped as if nothing as if
Existed no implements of harm

As a child sat by Long Island Sound on a particular rock & now
Irretrievable

& now it is of myself I feel compelled

Glowing in the dark some sort of branch bright ellipses running
Toward the rocking sea

How many times did I behold the ship its billowing its treasures its
Sentences of hard gold

Pick up any book & it is all written down

Everything returns to the sleep of itself

Buddha

There was a man came up to my bed in a green shadow. The shadow
enfolded him so that a glimpse presented only a cufflink but I was
very young

Behold myself

waving a stick in the air in order to examine the lost bright trails.
Like anyone my age spied creatures in dust avenues, also a Buddha in
a cave on the landing beckoned me under the stairs

So laughing I thought at me

My little being I can still feel it

Limbo Babies, a History

1

This fall, 25 more babies will be relegated to Limbo according to
Sister Mary Frances. We sat in the back row drawing a tree, a heart,
a man with a moustache while in Limbo 25 babies floated in a mist.
Disembodied is how we saw them, a little sad, thinner than usual
babies, bald—

& then the bell rang. Sister Mary Frances shook her nun's
sleeves. Her glasses held the glint of scissors. The Limbo Babies

just floated around
for Eternity: no spelling,
no dinner, no homework.

2

After a while they crept into our dreams. One wore a red jacket.
One had a pierced ear. One had been eating an Almond Joy.
We had been living our ordinary lives, walking up &
down streets, trying to make friends. Our mothers
kept driving off in cars. The heads of tulips
shattered in a wind storm.

When a cloud passed overhead we doubted its existence.

We wanted more out of life, more than the green Schwinn bicycle,
more than our parents' silverware & the front yard maple. Suspended
in a milky fog the Limbo Babies

followed us everywhere
& there was nothing we could do about it
except pray.

3

Like soldiers arranged in rows wearing spikes & epaulettes saluting
the flag. There is Innocence & there is its corollary, Greed.

After a while no one has anything left since each day exacts its fleshy
sliver.

Now we are even more bereft, alone with our crack-brained ideas,
wandering around, absently picking things up
linking arms with any old person . . .

always this exhaustion, as if the mist weren't enough to sustain
us, as if our encyclopedias had run out of descriptions
as if in the graveyards there weren't already
a plethora of zombies.

When the chalk settles over
the universe of landscapes
who will diagram our sentences?

4

Not jubilant today. They are in funk yawning & itching
& mumbling. They may be flu-ish or allergic

to olive trees. We are drawing bottles,
taking measurements with a pencil.

We are doing our math in a notebook
& writing paragraphs about Ancient Egypt. After a while

we will walk home & our father will shout at us.

Nothing makes sense. The ketchup is uncapped as is the scotch
& 2 times whatever is suddenly wrong.

In Ancient Egypt tombs were dark & airless & perfect. We are
always holding our breath. The moon spins in a socket.

We drench our eyes
in the useless air
but our tears still taste like salt.

5

Once again they have made an appearance & Sister Mary Frances
claims to be sympathetic even as she instructs us.

Poor little things she says & do we believe her? Some nice slanted
stream of light cascades across her black habit, its folds unfold
& fold again as she moves with a ruler, a piece of chalk,
an eraser. She moves to the board, then to the door
its chicken wire embedded in glass

she moves in & out of the light
in & out of the dust
in the light & we believe her.

Who Will

If you want me to sing if you want me to talk to you

The idea a shadow swept of muscle

The skin of the world searingly flayed

Things shudder inside things on & on

A person's tiny humming brain for instance

Nothing new: tall shuddering blue everywhere

Later in the restaurant the music made me cry

If you want me to stay here always or leave or die

You were still in a coma your blue eyes briefly

Polio

My mother became paralyzed then the family fell apart like the petals of a rose I used to blow on once. My room with organdy curtains & silver ribbon in the wallpaper, clumps of violets that through the years never faded like my heart. I say this only because after polio we turned around and never looked back. So it was the ragged hedges, the kitchen full of strangers. I had never been beautiful but now it was really so.

Shoes

Forced Oxford lace-ups too lazy to tie a knotty girl. In a shifting face a water face shudder I knew I knew believed I was mystical, perfected in a circle in a mystical circle under a tree keeping still. No clump clumping. Keeping still stones were thrown but never directed. Afraid to move.

Happiness

My first boyfriend bit his bottom lip when he danced with me that's
when I fell for him

My heart jumped around I felt my cheeks heat up
I knew I would remember

I wore a multicolored princess-line dress with velvet
lipstick to match my hair in a page boy

We danced shyly fingers touching by accident
not a beautiful couple we believed we found each other

Later on there was moonlight & making out we would not have
thought our love an addiction

He had pale blue eyes almost transparent lashes I felt his erection
through my dress I took it seriously a confession

One glows in the love of another one doesn't miss much
his hair fell over one eye

I tried to read the freckles on his shoulders all I want to do
he told me once is look into your eyes

After the summer we went our own ways in boarding school

The nuns kept his letters from me I never knew why

Eventually I'd get a page or two but they never made
sense without the rest

Strawberries & Cream

To have a friend was an occasion to feel strange & frozen in my white chair the white kitchen the white cream slow pour a breeze. Mother always a little nervous a little eat up & wash your hands & the mess was horrendous when Margie upchucked all over pink & white with a little sugar for a treat. A puddle a striped kind of pool spreading & rising up even now rising up.

Neccos

As sublime is finest thought in retrospect so Neccos can only be this very very sweetest in my wet hand squeezed delicious thing. God forgive my dirty nails my grime in all secrets & all my secrets my very dirty secrets Body of Necco. In the garden the boys fed our tongues & we girls gobbled, chocolate preferred. The licorice we disposed of—in trash or a pocket where they fizzed & slept.

prayer

Into the picture we scissor ourselves
Into the sweat of starched shirts
Into the life of the picture
Into the nest of trees behind the hill
Into the soft premises solid reckless leaves
Into the pointed shape of a house hanging cloudless
Into the room where the family
Into a future of small music
Into dismay no matter what hands
Into dismay running fast regardless
Into dismay silk mixed with dirt & flat sky
Into wands, angels, pigs' pink stupidity
Into the street is anyone there
Into dismay reckon & bleed the next thing vanish
Into this fast earth. Amen.

Beach Ball

Picnics were always possible in the same way that the goldfish pond was thought to go on forever with identical invisible-eyed orange fish. When the meat is turned the char-blistered smoke rising to the giant oak which these days is all bent over. The man wears a white coat and wields the long fork over our shining heads our shining heads bowed over the fish on the flagstone patio near the burgeoning shrubbery which consumes our beach ball, its heart still beating as it vanishes, green and yellow.

While My Guitar

My cousin likes to tell the story of how, when she used to visit me in
Pound Ridge, New York, my kids were always running around naked
while I read French poetry. We lived in a converted apple mill and
had a big yard, a wide flagstone terrace littered with toys and the kids
preferred to be naked, I believed, or else I was too absorbed in French
poetry to clothe them, which must have been my cousin's point

Who knows what I was reading? *Memory, memory, what do you want
of me? Autumn / makes the thrush fly through colorless air*
Oh Venus Oh Goddess! / I long for the days of antique youth . . .

Meanwhile, the children ran around naked, shrieking and laughing in
the garden hose wild spray or digging in the dirt with
my heirloom silver spoons and my littlest daughter
learned to arc her pee like a boy—standing up—
which thrilled us

Once a friend, a poet, catalogued the items she found on my stairway:
clumps of hair, orange peels, trail of paper clips

When I wore a black cape to a school conference, my son begged me
never to do that again. Do what? I said. You look like a witch, he said

Memory memory what do you want of me?

This longing a dazzled antique moon

Colorless the air of the future

Who were you on the bright flagstone, scooping up dolls and cars?
Write to me.

Nurse

The sand is tan. My towel is white, my bathing suit has triangles, my bucket is yellow. I am so tired of shoveling sand into the bucket. To watch the sailboats, to imagine myself walking across the gray water, like Jesus, is what I prefer. My companion is a large vague woman hardly sitting there beside me as if enshrouded in fog instead of flowery bathing suit with pleated skirt. Dripping mud on mud drips, imagine the terrible thrill. Theresa Theresa, that is all that's left of her wafting rose-petal presence, her scented-candle breath. Small hands all mine the afternoon of that day.

Tonight is

Tonight is a warmth spreading through my hair & eyes
Around me things whoosh & die
My scarves glow the skin on my arm touches the skin on my cheek
I am here   not going anywhere

On Seeing

When I was a kid, I wandered through the woods in Coventry, Connecticut, until I got lost. I was with my sister and we couldn't see, eventually, where we'd come from, nor could we see (or predict) the hermit's hut we stumbled on with its broken windows and torn mattress. This last fact impressed me particularly, the fact of the torn mattress, and I found myself imagining the vermin that shared the bed with the hermit, the tiny rats' tails that whipped around his eyelids at night, and I was also impressed with the fact of the hermit, who, in fact, we couldn't see, though I imagined him in vivid detail for my sister's edification– his malevolent face, his snarled beard and hair, the dagger shaking in his cruel bony fingers and pointing at our throats.

This would be one of the last walks I would take with my sister, not because either of us are incapacitated or dead, but because eventually my sister came to distrust me. I was an enthusiast for the hermit's hut and things of that nature. It excited me unreasonably to become lost in the woods, to pit my childish wits against the unknown and terrifying world, and it excited me even more to frighten my sister.

I couldn't see, at the time, the deep caves of estrangement that were forming in my sister's heart, and even when we found our way to the right path, the path that would take us back to our grandmother's house, even at that fortuitous turn of events, I couldn't see that luck was not a given in any life.

Years later a man is pointing out the constellations in a western sky and I can't see them. I can't see the Big Dipper, the Milky Way or Scorpio. The man is very patiently indicating how the Scorpion's tail curves through the sky, but all I see are many points of light all over everywhere in the black night, none distinguishable from the other by virtue of intensity or direction. Still, to be kind, I lie. I see, I say, though I can't see.

My mother always said I couldn't see the forest for the trees, but I don't see this as generally true of me, though it may have had some particular truth in the past, a time I can no longer see.

I often don't see how a certain thing comes to pass. For example, x may happen, then y, but to me there is no alphabetical progression, it might just as well have been x then l. It might just as well have been e then c.

I don't see why, between intimate acquaintances, estrangement eventually surfaces, as if it had been there all along, hiding and out of sight. I know I play a part in this estrangement, but I don't see what it is.

The things we see are always less interesting than the things we can't see, but when we eventually do see the latter, they, too, join the ranks of the uninteresting.

One almost never sees regret galloping along in the distance—it is its nature. Whereas the nature of love is to appear and disappear, like a magician's rabbit.

Sometimes, when concocting a meal without my glasses on, I can't see the salt pouring invisibly from carton to pot. On the other hand, when I cook while wearing glasses, they fog up so that I can't see the sautéing onions, the steaming vegetables.

Today in the grocery store, I didn't see the man barreling along behind me, nor apparently did he see me when he rammed his cart into my heel, causing it to bleed. Nor did I see my own blood leaving a spotty, macabre trail throughout the aisles, marking my route from produce to laundry detergent.

Some gaze deep, deep into the blackest night and see the lost future in stars that have ceased to exist. Who could believe this?

War, murder, the torture of prisoners—all take place way past my line of vision, offstage, and so perhaps I do not believe any of it. The invisible plots against us, the destiny of a village which at one moment is full of busy, reasonably happy citizens: a kid carrying a bag of groceries, a man on a bike, a colony of dogs, a woman with dark eyes gazing dreamily through her kitchen window at the precise moment the sky bursts into flame . . .

We should have left bread crumbs, I told my sister that day in the woods, but we should have left blood.

Uncle

How true that we spend the rest of our lives trying to recover who we thought we were as children. Far away a pond a jagged circle under the waning sun. Interposed rows of trees interposed a bench swing with two facing seats in green. Where a little scab of paint comes loose reveals the white flesh of metal. Nothing else from that era except the tall uncle whose glasses glint so that we think he is eyeless & blind.

Sleep, 1972

Wearing patched jeans & a man's hunting cap for effect, I showed up
at the Public Assistance offices, somewhere in
Mount Kisco, New York

Who was I trying to impress? I had two-year-old Rachel in one arm,
a big floral shopping bag containing a box of pastels, a book
or two of poetry, a novel, diapers in the other

We'd hitchhiked there, on the New England
Thruway, an old woman picked us up in her Oldsmobile

She had thin, tan hair & as we crept along, decades under the speed
limit, she gripped the wheel fiercely, as if maneuvering a tugboat over
a mountain

From the backseat I took in the sad color of her scalp,
I was worried for her.
Do you always pick up hitchhikers? I asked

At which she stiffened, so I shut up & closed my eyes

. . .

I was always tired. In the mornings, after the kids caught the school
bus, I'd crawl back into bed with the baby

After a day spent reading or staring at the frozen lake
I'd be exhausted again

The kids
returning from school wore me out, so did dinnertime & bedtime

I was tireder than tired trees, losing my leaves in my late 20s
Tireder than the lake's frozen, dormant surface
I was dead to the world

As I slept the ice-boaters raced by. They ran behind their boats
leapt on when the wind caught their sails the sound of them like
giant zippers zipping by entered my dreams . . .

. . .

In the welfare office I lit up Rachel beside me and god knows how
many other kids with their smoking parents

We blew the smoke around with abandon our kids already beyond
hope, they were used to it, their snow suits, even their little heads
reeking of nicotine

There was a woman
with a sore leg sitting nearby; she was all bandaged up,
her child wearing a hat
completely obscured his face,
rocked in a stroller

A thin girl with a resolving black eye
fidgeted with the loops of her jacket.
The black eye
was beautiful

purples and golds shot through with
turquoise flame

Her other eye brown and calm stared ahead trancelike

On the wall signs advised us of our rights
to patiently wait our turns have our IDs handy
use birth control

A few magazines lay around but they never transported me anywhere

Shadows Overcome

shadows overcome the living room

a silence so stirred I might drown in it

tv screen waves of quiet lights

likewise love a miracle

we enter & exit

me overcoming a thought

where thou art not desolation

out of nothing

Flight

A man reaches
under
a car &

removes
a bird.
Broken wing.

I hadn't seen

the bird
I'd been looking
up

at other birds cutting
like razors
across

my line of vision.
Which reminds me of

Un Chien Andalou
where a man slits
a woman's eyeball
& the vitreous

humor spills
out. It would be,
I was thinking

metaphorically,
like perception
spilling out—

The bird agitates
in the man's
cupped hand

then settles down.
Certain birds—the blackbird
for one—make nests

shaped like cups
so the man's hand
is a nest.

All the while the man is talking
—what we will eat for breakfast
—how good the sun feels

as if there were no
bird trembling there, as if he'd
never reached

with one unbroken sweep
under the car
to rescue it.

I should have been looking down—

There reside
blue & orange
Faro cigarette packages
bottle caps with stars

tiny discarded plastic
toys to slip
into a pocket
avec stones.

The bird—yellow beak
long tail feathers—
once or twice opens its

mouth as if to join
the conversation
then thinks better of it.

Kohlrabi

Strange & so an affinity. The knobby head, the layers, shucked & hidden, something inside uglier. Low stout cultivar German turnip, a kind of green though not so green it dazzles the spectator.

Apple Butter

Outside wind howls branches scrape all all is perilous & wet. What shaking house is this what shaking shaken house in which the girls one two sit & smear apple butter onto monks' bread/bread of secret.

Lost in the Woods

We got lost in the woods, my sister & me, me & my sister, I me myself lost with my sister in the woods the snatched jagged trees overhead the little wimpy birds futile bleat above our fright danger creep under rock & leaf. Lost in the woods oh help help blessed mother when it darkened up my hands froze my sister cried your fault. The wind singing all my fault all my fault when at last the fanged creature dragged us away & gave us a recipe for burning.

Footsteps Redux

I recall
Listening for your arrival
Cracking blossoms to bursting

The mountain over which sprays
Akin to starlight
Movie stars in halos
Monks in hoods

~

I recall
Hours of waiting
Details laborious & thin
Sounds in sequence
Light spread delicate

Every passage a suffer

Back to There

In the 20th century I piloted a toy plane to Russia. I'd been vacationing in Miami with my children who were very young. I had brown hair.

Much as I loved the beaches in Florida their display of golden bodies, the humming frothy waves, the turquoise sky, the sweet limpets' interiors of pearl, I harbored a craving for a dark city with elaborate architecture, men in ushankas.

Those days the regular airline that flew to Russia was called BOAC & Russia was called the USSR.

Once there I was dazzled by the gloom that presided over everything—
even the dogs skulked along gloomily
& the buildings, tragic with history, solemn as nuns . . .

Nor were the men & their hats a disappointment . . .

I found it all pleasurable
& strange. I sang

Ho Yeah
Ho Yeah
Ho Ho yeah

but I had to get back
to the kids. I was thin in those days
& not terribly strong.
I flew the toy plane back to Miami
but that part of the story is fuzzy, as if it'd
never happened.

It was hard raising those children
on my own. It was the 20th century—
I don't think we ever
stayed in a hotel. We were poor.
Once we drove to Florida to visit my parents
& it rained.

I Wanted

I wanted so much of everything then paused
Space equals longing longing equals what we thought we wanted
At the moment the room darkens

Just as the sky cowers to alert us in such a mood we could
Write our names across the
Wall but who will hear?

Dear Reader

For a while I was part of everything
Blue song low sky wind birds

Father pulled up the driveway his big Buick Electra gleaming
like an eye   Mother in the backyard crossword puzzle on her lap

Next door a swing set
Wendy's Tudor with the rock garden

The big brown house where Margie lived
Always calling me from the asphalt driveway

Dear Reader

So much is torn away

It is eerie to come back to the place one has left behind

The years go by in a dream nothing clasps me

Green furniture trimmed with gold leaf

A wallpaper of silver ribbons bouquets of fading flowers

My memories are like daisy chains that have been broken

An organdy curtain hushed the world

The remaining fragments are vivid

I am afraid of the quiet

This quiet time among artifacts
so much like nightmares
I feel my shoes sinking

Error

Too much green. Heavy the smell of green. Green air in which beings of green float in greenness. Angling toward green, I spy the creature, its mouth a gaping green hole extending to the first green, the green of greens. I will follow wherever I follow, I will want what I want. This is the lesson of green.

Too much green. Many trees scramble above our heads. Each grass blade a testimony. We always thought shadows were most like ghosts but we were wrong. Mother sits in the yard brightly surrounded.

The trees' upper parts are languid

dark clumps that move into the eye of this room so quietly
I almost forgot them

a rug is here a chair a stack of books a saucer / / /

                                                                  if you were
truly nearby I would feel you rustle just as the neighbor rustles out to
her garbage in her long skirts

Come Back to Me

My friend Martha believes when
She's not there she doesn't exist for people

& just because I'm not talking about you,
Mr. Tree, just because I can't hear you crash

On the forest floor, does that mean?
The same is true of all the wars

I never fought in. Blood, gunpowder, bodies smoldering
On rice paddies that dizzy adrenalin

Rush in a fighter plane I can almost imagine
It was me. Silly girl.

Remember the body count?
The tv news the tv news

Ghoulishly there
& not there battlefields & soldiers
In the fake mahogany RCA frame

Other props included
Stereo, stack of LPs
My dad's dish of ice cream

Or my kids leaping up to change
The channel back to *The Flintstones*
Wilma always looked so worried—

Better Wilma than Martha or me.
I was looking anywhere for inspiration, Dear
The underside of a leaf

Struck me as miraculous
Possibly not seen by any other human eye
But so what?

Dinner

Dinner was beef and a shined knife crystal silver linen tablecloth so draped precisely so slivered so round. Instinctively I knew I knew everything including glass bowl with floating posy doily made of lace. Instinctively I knew faces composed of ravenous & shut, bitter & cool. Lima bean pallor in a bowl. Roast crust makes red only smaller & lovely fabulous beige popping blisters. I didn't know myself but everything else had beauty & sound.

Selma's Soufflé

Buffeting clouds in a flurry of ahhs & oohs. Little wormholes in the table horse chestnut color & as gleamed. Doilies under fingerbowl pools, faintly blue. Faintly troubled with bits of apricot. The spoon makes the nicest cave. Entirely satisfying breakthrough. Vanilla sauce warm as a blanket.

There Is a Blankness behind All This Noise

a blind way of seeing ::

in the heart a ratcheting bolts loosened leaves everywhere

could be that smell predominates the ear stunned in the burden of air
                    in the pebbled path beside the orange globe mallow

String Beans

With mushroom soup my mother never out of step. Oh and it was *divine,* her word, the green and the off-white, breadcrumbs' yellow crust crackling like a mud yard sun-baked. There I buried my gold signet ring digging deep as China & flinging hard. No thud. No miraculous sinkage. You could put anything anywhere a casserole or a garden.

A drumroll & planets will rotate

as simply as a glass turned on its side the flowers that have spilled from it the small glistening pool of water no bigger than an eye who sees what stares into it

Ob la di ob la da—

"I used to lie around & get stoned
with Desmond that's when I remember
hearing that song for the first time
Desmond all he ever wanted to do is lie around & get stoned
& fuck women & he always had plenty of great weed"

What year was that?

"That was a million years ago. Before we met. Before
all the great tragedies of the 20th century"

How old?

"College age and dumb, but so happy we thought life
would go on & on"

Whatever happened to him?

"Who knows? I heard he met this beautiful woman and settled down
but by now everyone is divorced so who knows?"

Sad but true. Let's not get divorced.

"We can't if we don't marry"

Let's not ever marry.

"Time is running out—
The sky is closer than it used to be, the birds gouging out apricot
chunks summer after summer from that tree I planted 20 years ago"

A little plane creeps into a cloud and out again—if you turn your head you can see it, like last week

In the Yard

In the yard a man mowing

Reminds me of some dad not mine.

Also the bus throws us back to forsythia

To the empty wands the writer the waste of it all

Tumbling over our backs bicycles with us on each step

I forgot to call then remembered I remembered

Then went through a door

Inside

Now the brother's leg braces are so tiny and intricate they are like miniature chain saws. Wheelchair a sewing machine *zzz* as if the mother is stitching together each of our rooms, the better to shut us up. Rain dots. Green sofa with nubs always forbidden. Inside the house inside the brain looking out at the lawn the bicycle the squirrel. Behind the eye in its husk away from others' sharp masks, we beseechers.

I Didn't Know What to Do So

I didn't know what to do so I felt along the concepts of my skin

Knotholes, burrows, holes for snakes

A mirror whose spoke is calm

A white stand of aspen carved up by wind.

Between indifference & passion a shifting line, clouds like ducks' eggs, feathers incipient

Hills precisely out of earshot

The path holds its quotient of life

We walk (crunch)

Horse dung on a trail, a log or two crosses the view, a mountain worth gasping

Face

Within the face a welter such that horizon and very small sails out in front and the peculiar colors of rocks were all one by one enigmas. The strange face in its strange cave of hair. At one moment seem to be bobbing around. A natural way of thought there being no words then or now. Then or now in the welter of the self still wordless existence on a par with floating.

On Looking

In order to see a photograph well, it is best to look away
or close your eyes.
—Roland Barthes

(1)

a man turning his head

a stream with rocks in it

pine trees grow out of a crag

a book about x

a man wears a slight smile

a palm frond

a museum of fading things

the water between the trees

(2)

two people might choose to stand close together

one mood transferred to another

a woman in white with a scarf

the rocks in a book look like clouds

they are looking at the same thing

:: snow

boughs laden & monochrome

light travels along a forearm

(3)

no sky no sky whatsoever

reflections are smudged & vertical

two people are merely shapes

a view from a peak

she looks to him for a cue

a serious man wishes he were elsewhere

she is thin her sleeve ribbed with folds

a shadow interacts with another

(4)

the accidental is natural

the page is shining & full

image opposite image

the hatted man the friendly gaze

a brown hand a speckled rock

where will they go

a person looks away

they are always leaving

(5)

they are flickering stars through a telescope

a museum of lost things

they are mirrors laden & monochrome

still unravish'd

smudged boughs of x

like beholding the mute of a galaxy

it is both of them leaving

it is like looking at both of them leaving

Hands

My father was another story, red meat. Walked around in a silver dome of air hard and specialized the better to carve and devour. He liked his scotch on the rocks and various cigarette brands, didn't matter which. Golfing in those green pants and terrified of heights which should have made me soften. A memory of him fiddling with the knob of the car radio and another of his gold pinky ring on the banister, each of which involve large hands—a neat crop of hair pressed into every blessed knuckle.

His My Cushion

No promises were ever made. The window opened to the same view of trees. The noise of the air-conditioning sends a shiver. Behind all this you sense a wish for air. The blue of the book cover fades to green and the lettering is tall as if a man were walking across the pages or swimming with long angular arms. Soon he will enter. But enter what? So many names glitter the world, his my cushion, his my stationary pulse.

I amaze easily this

I amaze easily this you can say about me

mostly I am tired

the march of minutes akin to some painstakingly knitted
scarf

I remember counting them until you
arrived

then subtracting then multiplying myself
by the way you spoke

& the look on your face by
my anguish which I dis-
guised until I was
almost asleep

◆

When you came into my life I was sitting
the windows were closed
I could barely hear anything though I strained to

It was not unkindness that made me take
notice but amusement
& the type of green shadow you cast over my books

For Example

I may for eg chop an onion

Make the bed with fresh pillowcases

Hang a picture of the rusted virgin
  over the chest of drawers with the missing handle

Good-bye

long ago I left my ring in a taxi & that fact of my life
has directed every action
the leaving of things and people

ACKNOWLEDGMENTS

The author wishes to acknowledge the following publications, in which some of these poems have previously appeared: *Barrow Street, Fence, Seneca Review,* and *Quarterly West.*

Also, many thanks to dear friends and brilliant poets Brian Blanchfield, Barbara Cully, Shira Dentz, and Cynthia Hogue for their help and encouragement along the way. Big thank-yous to my editor, Martha Rhodes, for her masterful editing suggestions and for her belief in this book; to Four Way staff Ryan Murphy and Sally Ball for their expertise in all things; and to the indefatigable Martha Carlson-Bradley for her careful attention. And finally, thanks and love to my boyfriend, Steve Romaniello, who inspires me with his artistic stamina and always has my back.

Karen Brennan is the author of five books of varying genres, including poetry collections *Here on Earth* (1989) and *The Real Enough World* (2006), both from Wesleyan University Press; AWP Award–winning short fiction *Wild Desire* (University of Massachusetts Press, 1990); story collection *The Garden in Which I Walk* (Fiction Collective 2, 2005); and a memoir, *Being with Rachel* (Norton, 2001). Brennan is a recipient of a National Endowment for the Arts fellowship in fiction, and her fiction, poetry, and nonfiction have appeared in anthologies from Graywolf, Norton, Penguin, Spuytin Duyvil, University of Georgia, and University of Michigan, among others. She is professor emerita at the University of Utah and teaches in the MFA Program for Writers at Warren Wilson College. karenbrennan.org.

advance praise for *Confluence*

"A queer West Coast Bildungsroman, *Confluence* brings readers back to a time before Stonewall, and before Vancouver bristled with mirrored towers. The story it tells is as touching as the novel's provenance. It simply teems with love—the unrequited, the joyously consummated, and for the authors, love undying."
—CAROLINE ADDERSON, author of *A Russian Sister* and *A Way to Be Happy*

"This remarkable act of twin authorship transports you to the thrill of desire at the water's edge and to an intimacy almost too personal to bear. It's a reminder that what hides something can also reveal it spectacularly. Run to *Confluence*. It will give you a lifetime of goosebumps."
—DANIEL ALLEN COX, author of *I Felt the End Before It Came*

"*Confluence* is a gushing hot spring of a novel, swirling with sex, self-discovery, and stories that bubble up to insist on being told. In its pages, gay men find community—and communion—through honouring the desires that bind them across vast distances of geography and time. Don't miss this exquisitely unique and heart-wrenchingly beautiful book."
—MATTHEW J. TRAFFORD, author of *Runs in the Blood*

"*Confluence*, co-authored by Lucian Childs and his late husband, Alex Turner, is a gift. Many stories are held within this novel: a daring, taboo coming of age; an homage to the beautiful BC wilderness; a lively, little-known piece of queer Canadian history. Written with great care and feeling, it is also testament to a love between two men that transcends the ephemeral; I am heartened by their courage."

—KRISTYN DUNNION, author of *Stoop City*

"*Confluence* captures beautifully the pre-Stonewall moment, but more than that, it is a vivid record of the time in a young queer person's life where desire is all and yearning, fear, and confusion are at their most powerful. It brings to mind the novels I searched for and rarely found as a queer kid, when I needed to see how other people had lived through it. A loving, warm, and turbulent page-turner."

—RICHARD MIRABELLA, author of *Brother & Sister Enter the Forest*